Methods & Mechanics Companion Book

by Todd Sucherman and Brad Schlueter

CREDITS

Methods & Mechanics Companion Book
by Todd Sucherman and Brad Schlueter

Transcriptions and Music Engraving by Brad Schlueter

Executive Producers: Paul Siegel and Rob Wallis

Edited by Joe Bergamini

Design and Layout by Rick Gratton

Audio Recorded by J.R. Taylor

Photos by Eric Dorris, Scott Cavender and Ash Newell

Catalog HDBK30/HL321269
ISBN10: 1458417387

INSIDE THIS BOOK

ABOUT THE DISC ◉

Track Page Contents

FOREWORD

Hey Mom, I wrote a book! Well, sort of, I suppose. Not the kind she'd like, but I'm sure (being the supportive mother she's always been) she'll think it's "very nice."

Really, most of the heavy lifting here was done by Brad Schlueter, who spent an insane amount of hours transcribing the ideas I played on the *Methods and Mechanics* DVD. I must confess here and now (in my own book no less) that I've never been one to devour drum books. I've been mostly an eyes-and-ears guy who never had the talent to transcribe or read detailed drum notation. Now, I can read, of course, but on the thousands of sessions I've done, most of the charts were lead sheets or had drum notation guides only there for interpretation. Only a handful of times was I ever presented charts with detailed full kit notation. I remember meeting Steve Michaud when I spent my one year at Berklee in Boston. Steve is one of the greatest drummers on the planet, and back then he showed me his book of all these incredible Vinnie Colaiuta transcriptions from live Zappa bootlegs, and I was astounded by his ability to do that. I wished I had that gift. I still do. Brad Schlueter has the same transcribing gift, and we have known each other since the early '90s. I feel he has been very familiar with my playing over the years and has been the perfect collaborator for this project. I've received so many requests for a transcription companion book for the *Methods and Mechanics* DVD, and thanks to Hudson Music, Brad Schlueter, and you, the reader, it's now here in your hands.

It has been interesting revisiting material that was filmed and recorded in late 2007 right at a time when I am now in the editing stages for the *Methods and Mechanics II: Life on the Road, Songs, Solos, Stories and Lessons* DVD. To me, the materials here contain more than just notes on a page. They contain the culmination of every gig I've ever done, every teacher I had, and every wonderful musician I've ever played with.

I feel that it's our duty to pass on information to the next generation. That's what makes drummers so unique: our willingness to share. We are a large group of friends—it's the greatest club on earth. The *Methods and Mechanics* DVD has been one of the most rewarding, humbling, and gratifying experiences of my life, and it's my hope that these materials inspire creativity in your playing and thinking. I also hope the entire *Methods and Mechanics* series helps guide you musically and conceptually through your career as a working musician.

Todd Sucherman
(On a tour bus traveling to Glasgow from Manchester)
June 2011

INTRODUCTION

Methods and Mechanics is a breakthrough drum DVD. While it reflects Todd's depth of technique, musicality and experience, it was primarily designed to educate and motivate the viewer. This it does quite well. In fact, it's packed with rudimental and double bass technique exercises, songs, solos, and lots of tips and career advice of what being a professional drummer is all about. The production quality is also higher than many other drum DVDs to date, offering plenty of camera angles to see exactly what Todd is playing. The stories and footage of Todd's life on the road are something many drummers might have dreamt about, but rather than just offer the fantasy, he goes into exactly what it takes to become the kind of drummer other musicians will want to hire. It is also perfect for drummers who simply want to be inspired by one of today's finest players.

I was very happy to be asked to transcribe and co-write this book partly because I have known Todd for a couple of decades and am very familiar with his drumming. As excellent and thorough as the DVD is, many of the patterns Todd plays are so advanced they could perplex any drummer. Frankly, lots of them perplexed me at first. This book gave me the opportunity to decipher his playing both for myself and other ambitious drummers. After all, Todd has tons of licks, and some of them go by at a ridiculous speed. If you heard something in a song or solo and didn't know exactly what Todd was doing, we think you'll find this book to be the perfect companion piece to the DVD.

Brad Schlueter

ABOUT TODD SUCHERMAN

2009 saw Todd Sucherman win the *Modern Drummer* Reader's Poll for #1 Rock Drummer and #1 Educational DVD with *Methods and Mechanics*, as well as #1 Clinician in *DRUM!* Magazine, all while touring the world with multi-platinum group Styx and performing drum clinics and recording sessions from coast to coast. But his musical history began basically at birth.

Todd Sucherman grew up in a musical family. His father, Arnold J. Sucherman was a doctor by day and a big band drummer by night. He was the house drummer at the famed Chez Paree in Chicago through the 1940s and '50s. During that time he worked with Lena Horne, Sammy Davis Jr., Sophie Tucker, Joe E. Lewis, Jack Benny, and countless others. While on the road, at a gig in New Orleans, Arnold met a young actress, Jo Seiwert, who was performing in the same variety show. They were married and soon formed a family of their own.

Paul was first (keyboards), then Joel (bass), then Todd (drums). Todd was fascinated with the drums as an infant. His father taught him to play and he could read music by age five. His first paying gig was with his brothers ("The Sucherman Brothers") at age six. They continued to play together and with other musicians for years.

Todd kept up with his musical studies through school and attended Berklee College of Music for one year. There he studied privately with Gary Chaffee, a world-renowned educator whose students included Steve Smith and Vinnie Colaiuta.

In 1988, Todd returned to Chicago and quickly established himself as a first-call musician on the recording scene. An in-demand player for live and session work, he soon formed an association with the band Styx. Todd was called in to record when Styx's original drummer John Panozzo was ill. After Panozzo's untimely death, Todd's position in the band was solidified. Sixteen years later, Styx continues to play to million's of fans all over the world, averaging 100 dates a year. Todd has recorded several albums with the band, including *Big Bang Theory,* which put the band in the top 50 on Billboard for the fourth straight decade. In between his time with Styx, Todd has recorded over 1000 radio and TV spots and worked with artists diverse as Peter Cetera, Brian Culbertson, Spinal Tap, Michael Bolton, The Falling Wallendas, Eric Marienthal, and Brian Wilson (including his 2003 release with Paul McCartney, Eric Clapton and Elton John). Todd has also been an in-demand clinician, performing at drum festivals around the world.

In 2007 Todd produced and played on the debut from Taylor Mills, *Lullagoodbye,* which featured appearances from Brian Wilson and Tommy Shaw.

After years of touring and recording, Sucherman began work on his much-anticipated instructional DVD release, *Methods and Mechanics* (available from Altitudedigital.com). In this presentation—which *Modern Drummer* magazine called "a stunning achievement" and "one of the most stunning looking and sounding DVDs ever"—Sucherman brings the knowledge of thousands of gigs, shows and recording sessions along with over three decades as a professional drummer to this useful and unique DVD package. Astonishing technique, power, and musicality explode from the various musical and solo performances throughout this presentation. Working with artists over a myriad of genres diverse as Styx, Brian Wilson, Spinal Tap, Eric Marienthal, Peter Cetera, John Wetton, Steve Cole, The Falling Wallendas and many more, there's a wealth of knowledge imparted that goes way beyond just the technical aspects of drumming. *Methods and Mechanics* is filled with practical career tips that will help you navigate through the music business as well as mental aspects and cerebral approaches to the art of playing music on the drums. Filmed in 16X9 in high definition at a stunning location, this DVD features music from Styx, Taylor Mills, and Jerry Goodman, and contains various solos and playing examples in an array of styles as well as technical lessons to enhance your rhythmic and musical vocabulary.

ABOUT BRAD SCHLUETER

Brad Schlueter is a busy professional drummer, drum teacher, music writer and transcriber. He has contributed hundreds of articles to *Drum!* magazine and has also written for *Electronic Musician*, *Modern Drummer*, and *JazzTimes* magazines as well as for Vic Firth, Gearwire and Thomann music and many other websites. He absolutely loves the drums and will foolishly play just about any gig offered him. He holds a bachelor's degree from N.I.U., and peculiarly spent nearly a decade competing as a rudimental snare drummer in the University of Chicago and Chicago Caledonian Pipe Bands. We suspect he either liked wearing the kilt or has a thing for redheaded women.

More Background On Todd

I had heard of Todd long before I met him or had the chance to see him play. Musicians I respected kept bringing his name up asking if I'd heard of him or seen him play yet. I knew he must be good because there was an unmistakable awe in their voices, plus adjectives like "unfreakinbelievable" kept popping up. The first time I heard him was on a track while at Solid Sound Studios. I had shown up early for a session with the late, great Phil Bonnet, while one of the other engineers was finishing up a rough mix from another session. While I listened to the playback, the drumming immediately caught my ear. It wasn't anything obvious like a blistering fill or insane polyrhythm; it was a couple of subtle things he had played. One was a tasteful hi-hat embellishment and the other was the graceful way he had come out of chorus and brought the dynamic down for the next verse. I asked who it was and I was stunned that it was this same teenager that I had kept hearing about—stunned not from his chops, but by his musicality and the maturity of his approach. I briefly wondered, "Is it too late to take up the bass?"

The first time I actually saw Todd play was when we were both in the finals of a drum solo contest held at the long-gone Avalon nightclub. I had still never heard Todd play live, let alone solo. To this day, I am ever so grateful to whoever was responsible for scheduling my solo to occur before his. Had it been the other way around, I might have snuck out the back door of the club after seeing him tear up the kit. From about that point on, Todd and I became friends based on our mutual love of all things drum-related.

I saw Todd play with lots of his early bands: fusion bands, rock bands, the Falling Wallendas, the China Club house band, and many others. I remember seeing him in a large samba band while I was on a first date at a restaurant. I kept peering over the poor girl's shoulder to watch Todd play, repeatedly losing track of whatever she was saying. (The rest of the date didn't go so well.) I attended some of his first clinics and saw him win the Guitar Center drum-off three years in a row. I think they made him a judge after that since no one in Chicago could beat him, and that is saying a lot. If you will pardon a little hometown bragging, Chicago has always had more than its share of superb drummers.

Todd has always been a gracious and supportive friend, talking drums and drummers, having me sit in at his China Club gig, and subbing out gigs to me occasionally when he was double booked. I currently play in a couple bands with trumpeter/bassist/bandleader Pete Fleming, who played with Todd and his older brothers in a band, starting from when Todd was just 10 years old, and continuing until he went away to attend Berklee. He told me how they had to carry his drums and trap case into gigs because Todd was too little to manage them on his own. At that age, I would take my kit to the annual school talent show—while Todd had already begun his career as a working professional.

The first time I transcribed some of Todd's drumming was back in his Falling Wallendas days. He has always been a fruitful drummer to analyze. He just has so much good stuff, and so much of it is completely unique to him. Of course, he has influences. You can hear echoes of drummers like Steve Smith, Vinnie Colaiuta, Tony Williams, and many others in him, but Todd is not a clone of anyone, having developed a strong individual voice of his own at an early age.

In these pages you will frequently see an accented snare followed by two or more ghost notes. One thing that differentiates Todd from any of the other hundred-plus drummers I have transcribed is his use of the Moeller/velocity stroke and rebounded grace notes. Sure, ghost notes are nothing new. Many drummers find the "Purdie shuffle" (named after the great session drummer Bernard Purdie) challenging to master because there is a loud backbeat immediately followed by a ghost note. The superb Jeff Porcaro combined the Purdie shuffle with the Bo Diddley beat and John Bonham's half-time shuffle on Led Zeppelin's "Fool In The Rain" to create his signature groove on Toto's song "Rosanna." When Todd plays shuffles, he often plays two ghost notes after the backbeat, creating sort of a Purdie/Porcaro shuffle *on steroids*.

Todd employs this same technique for much of his rock playing. Those extra notes may not seem important since many may be nearly inaudible. Most drummers either couldn't or wouldn't play them, probably deeming them unnecessary, but I have found they add an interesting texture and energy to his playing that I have never heard from another "rock" drummer. Of course, he is more than just a rock drummer, and is capable of just about any style you can name. Like many professional drummers, Todd often plays his cymbals accenting every other note. This combined with the numerous ghost notes creates some interesting hills and valleys in his dynamics that may not be obvious at first, but—like his predecessors Bernard Purdie and Jeff Porcaro—make even the simplest grooves he plays feel so much deeper.

Many drummers may be blinded by Todd's obviously ridiculous chops and overlook how well he dramatizes the emotional moods of the music he plays. His musicality, more than his chops, is what I believe is responsible for his continued success. Chops without musicality are worthless to the people that hire drummers. Without his musical ability, all the thousands of gigs and sessions that helped him ascend his career ladder would not have happened.

That said, I confess I have loved checking out Todd's playing over the years both to admire his skills and to steal licks and ideas. Todd would correct me on this point, saying, "You don't have to steal them—they're free." There are a lot of ideas in this book, and though they are not exactly free, I hope that if you learn a couple licks, ideas, or gain a little insight into one of today's finest drummers, you'll find this book well worth the investment. Since I am also a drum teacher, I will be analyzing some of the patterns that struck me as notable in my commentaries to help you find things of interest, as well as ones you might like to add to your own playing. I hope you find this book helpful in your quest to become a more interesting and musical drummer.

TRANSCRIPTION NOTES

A transcriber's job is to translate a musical performance into notation. A rule of thumb with very complex performances is to "eschew obfuscation." Go ahead; look it up, we'll wait. Transcription is at best an approximate science. If one were to try to notate in exact detail every aspect of a complex performance, the resulting notation would be so cumbersome that it would not illuminate much more than it would obscure, resulting in the dreaded "black page" phenomena. There are infinite levels of dynamics, nuances of articulation, and variations in timing that if correctly notated by a computer, would result in indecipherable gibberish, unless you happen to enjoy the challenge of reading double-dotted 64th notes. That is good news for every music transcriber's continued employment prospects.

When transcribing from video we gain the advantage of seeing what and how a musician is playing a piece. One obvious advantage is that this allows for the inclusion of stickings and footings, which makes this book far more valuable to drummers wishing to gain a deeper understanding of the techniques employed, or for those who want to add a few more brilliant licks to their repertoire.

For this book, I tried not to interpret or remove anything intelligible from Todd's spectacular performances. I set the threshold of notes I would include in these pages lower than many transcribers would so they only affect the quietest, most indecipherable notes and best represent Todd's playing without including incidental strokes. Hopefully drummers wishing to get an accurate representation of his playing will find this more detailed approach valuable.

Many of the fills and some of the beats have stickings notated under them to help you learn how Todd has played specific patterns. While uppercase R and L indicate right hand or left hand, sometimes the stickings will be in lower case, which is used for the grace note of a flam. At other times you will see a B, R/L or L/R written beneath a note. These stickings are used to indicate the hands playing in unison. The B is a more general indication and simply means "both hands." R/L is more specific indicating the right hand plays the note higher on the staff and the left hand plays the lower one. L/R means the opposite. So a crash played with the right hand and a snare being played with the left hand will be notated R/L since the crash is written above the snare on the staff.

You have probably noticed that there is a great deal of notation in this book. Most of this book is written in one layer meaning all the beams go upwards. There is a simple and practical reason for this. Writing the book in two layers would have increased the page count substantially since fewer staves would have fit per page, resulting in more harvested trees and raising the cost of the book. However, I used two layers for brief spots when I felt it was necessary to clarify a very complex pattern.

Occasionally, you may see something like "hi-hat continues" used to keep the transcriptions more readable and avoid filling the page up with repeating parts that could obscure the focal point of what Todd is expressing.

In case you are interested in pursuing a lucrative career as a drum transcriber, whether for the babes or the glamour of it all, and were wondering what it is like to transcribe material as complex as this, the brilliant comedian Steven Wright has a joke that goes: "It's a small world, but I wouldn't want to have to paint it." The longest solo contains almost 12,000 elements: notes, articulations, dynamics and stickings, etc. Monks would probably make good music transcribers.

Drum Key

There are two different keys depending on whether Todd played his jazz kit (with three ride cymbals) or his big rock kit (with up to three snare drums). Eventually, after debating the matter with myself, I chose to put the notes on their traditional place on the staff but decided to use three different note heads to indicate which instrument was being played. I tried to be somewhat consistent in the notation of both kits. I used a traditional oval note head for his main snare, which is located furthest to the right of the three, and a standard "x" note head for the flat ride cymbal furthest to his right. The middle snare received a black triangular note head as did the middle ride cymbal, and the one located to the left of the others received a hollow (or white) triangular note head. Other possibilities presented themselves and none was completely satisfactory. A couple of pieces have x-shaped note heads on tom lines, which indicate that tom rims were played.

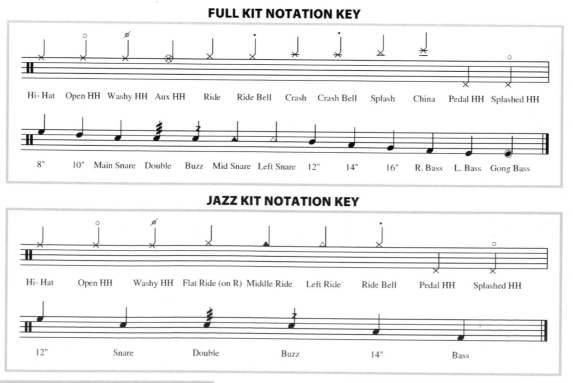

FULL KIT NOTATION KEY

Hi-Hat, Open HH, Washy HH, Aux HH, Ride, Ride Bell, Crash, Crash Bell, Splash, China, Pedal HH, Splashed HH

8", 10", Main Snare, Double, Buzz, Mid Snare, Left Snare, 12", 14", 16", R. Bass, L. Bass, Gong Bass

JAZZ KIT NOTATION KEY

Hi-Hat, Open HH, Washy HH, Flat Ride (on R), Middle Ride, Left Ride, Ride Bell, Pedal HH, Splashed HH

12", Snare, Double, Buzz, 14", Bass

SONG TRANSCRIPTIONS

TEARS OF JOY

TODD:

I first became aware of Jerry Goodman's "Tears of Joy" on his live album from 1987 called *It's Alive*. About a decade later, Jerry and I became friends, and at some point in 2004 I asked him if he would record the track for me. On the original live record, the rhythm section of Jim Hines (drums) and Bob Lizik (bass) usually stated the downbeat (beat 1) of the groove regularly. When Jerry sent me his track, there were many bars where the bass resolution was actually placed on the anticipation: beat 13. This changed the rhythmic shape tremendously, and I asked Jerry about it. He simply replied, "That's how I originally wrote it." Who was I to mess with it? This made navigating through the track more difficult at first—but ultimately more interesting.

Try to internalize the different ways to subdivide 13 by breaking them down into groups of 3s and 2s, such as: **2-2-3-3-3** / **2-2-3-2-2-2** / **3-3-3-4**

BRAD:

Playing in 13 would be a nightmare for most drummers, so it is all the more impressive that Todd manages to do so with such apparent ease and incredible musicality, especially at such a brisk tempo. Todd enters this song with some delicate cymbal work before launching into the main groove in 13/8. For this song, I tried to beam the eighth notes to indicate the phrasing of the patterns within the 13/8 time signature. For example, bar 23 can be thought of as subdivisions of 2-2-3-3-3. However, I combined the 2-2 phrases, writing them as a grouping of 4 (4-3-3-3), since it is a little easier to read that way. Who doesn't need a little help when reading 13/8? At bar 72, Todd plays a new groove on his toms that has a different phrasing, and the beaming changes to 3-3-3-4.

There are some clever fills in the track worth checking out. Bar 36 has a nice cymbal fill that uses some paradiddle-diddles and a paradiddle. One of the advantages of using a rudiment over single strokes for fills like this is that singles tend to sound somewhat flat, whereas a rudimental sticking usually has a dynamic shape that often sounds more musical. Todd throws in a killer flam fill in bar 57. For this one, his left hand has to play continuously while his right accents the toms. There are many different types of flams and this is a good example of a "drumset" flam. Todd often plays them this way: accenting the grace notes of flams and placing them on toms, which differs from the traditional snare drum approach of playing grace notes very low and softly.

In bar 104 there is a ride cymbal and snare written together with a "z" on the stem of the note. This refers to a snare buzz, not a cymbal buzz or unison buzz and that will be the case throughout this book. Bars 106 and 170 show Todd playing a unison variation of a pattern known as a "blushda" (rL RRL) between his ride and snare while he splashes his hi-hat. Bar 129 has a jarring polyrhythmic snare fill where Todd plays four over three (four notes played in the space of three eighth notes) twice.

Bars 142 through 147 show two absolutely mind-boggling polyrhythmic fills that Todd plays perfectly. The first would be a very cool fill that would fit nicely in 4/4 if played as 16th-note triplets. How he fit 24 eighth notes to fit into the space of 13 demonstrates his utter command of odd times. He follows it up with a faster fill that is equally unusual. This one has three ten-note groupings of 8 single-stroked notes played with the hands over two bass drum notes that (again) he magically fits within the 13/8 time signature. Another unique (but this time far easier) pattern occurs in bar 162. Here, he plays a descending tom fill with his right hand while his left hand doubles each note with a crash. The final insane fill in this song begins in bar 186 and may be the hardest one simply because he keeps shifting gears throughout it.

TEARS OF JOY

METHODS and MECHANICS

ONE WITH EVERYTHING

TODD:

"One With Everything" was written for Styx's *Cyclorama* CD, and I think it's the definitive 21st-century Styx track. We all wrote this together from various nuggets. I remember diagramming the song form on a board at the rehearsal hall in LA, trying to get the form just right. I'm really proud of the playing and writing on this, and it still floats in and out of our live set.

BRAD:

When I first heard this tune I was blown away. Styx has always had progressive rock elements in their music, especially in that style's peak back in the '70s. This homage is true to the style, with its share of odd-time signatures, grandiose keyboards, interesting guitar parts and (of course), ridiculous drumming.

The opening fills announce that you are in for a wild ride. The intro beat is a funky groove with a hi-hat opening on the "ah" of 2 that every environmentally-conscious drummer should learn, since it can be recycled and used in lots of other songs. The fill at the end of bar 28 can be put to use elsewhere as well.

Todd plays his ride alternating between the bell and the shoulder of the cymbal. This technique creates a polyrhythmic feel when used in odd time signatures. During the choruses, Todd rides his crash with a Ringo-esque back-and-forth motion that creates a hint of swing. He also does a very subtle thing to help make the section sound grander: he crashes on beat one of every other bar but does not play the "&" after the crash. By letting the crash ring a little longer, he emphasizes the moment. Todd does this repeatedly and by design. You can also see him leading with his left foot on some of the double-bass patterns (bar 53), and using his right foot to fill in between them. Also, notice how many of his signature Moeller triple-stroked backbeats are played through this section. Todd shifts to a lower gear in bar 102 and plays an interesting and delicate cymbal pattern over a splashed hi-hat.

The fills contain hybrid rudiments that are normally reserved for drum corps or Scottish pipe-band competitions, like "cheeses" and "flam fives." "Quads" (RH LH RF LF), paradiddles, and paradiddle-diddles make appearances as well. Todd combines all these rudiments to create two perfectly musical and blistering fills that raise the bar for any drummer who attempts them.

If you would like to improve your hands but do not have a rudimental background, here are some of the rudiments used in these fills laid out for you, along with a couple of four-measure hand warm-ups/solos that are brief enough to be memorized and used before gigs.

Suggestion: Accent the paradiddles strongly. This will help the sticks rebound more quickly and help you gradually build up your speed. The second warm-up is much harder than the first so start slowly and be patient. Usually, the beginning of the cheeses and flam fives are accented, though for variety and different technical demands, you can also accent the last note.

"One With Everything" Rudiments

2 ONE WITH EVERYTHING

ANYTHING

TODD:

The main groove developed from the guitar and bass parts. It's sort of a tribal-sounding feel in the verses, where I'm playing the toms, the tom rims for random percussive sounds, and the snare drum with snares off. There's a deep shaker for the constant pulse to compliment the overall vibe of the feel. When the chorus hits—crash!—the snares pop on, there's ride cymbal, and the shaker goes away and becomes a bright tambourine—and then goes back to the shaker tribal groove two bars later, creating these "scene changes" between the sections. I'm thinking about reacting emotionally to the lyrics, building and shaping the song, propelling certain sections, and pulling things back in the right place. I'm looking to shape the track and support the various sections to give them their unique flavors.

BRAD:

This song features the very talented Taylor Mills on vocals. It has a remarkable and very unusual drum groove that—in spite of it's uniqueness—somehow fits the song like a glove. This tribal approach also works to set up the more conventional sections of the chorus, helping them to have more of a dramatic payoff. During the chorus, Todd uses his ride bell (indicated by the black dot above the cymbal) on the quarter notes.

There is a tasty flam fill in bar 22 that subtly sets up Taylor's next verse, and a ripping fill in bar 65 that kicks the last chorus up another notch. Todd's use of the rims adds an interesting percussive texture to this groove. The x-shaped note heads on the tom lines indicate which tom rim he plays.

ANYTHING

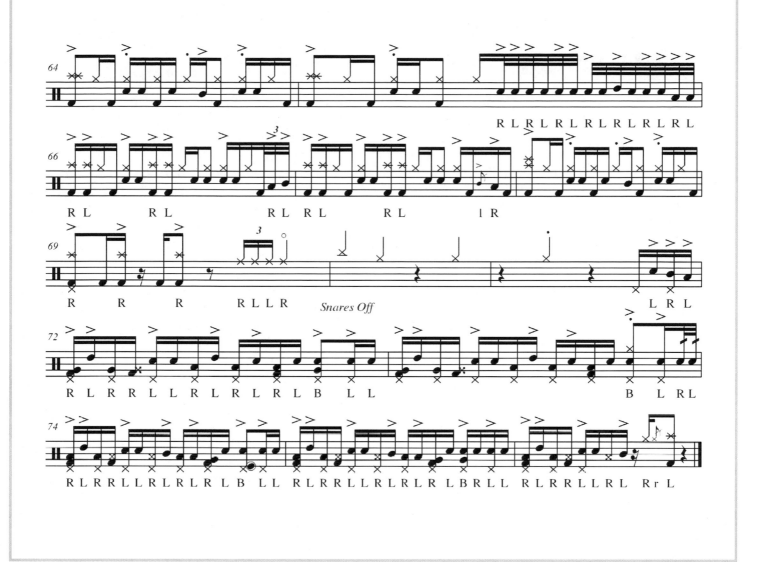

CENTER OF YOUR HEART

TODD:

I believe the song "Center of Your Heart" would have been a big hit in a parallel universe. Scott Bennett, the composer, is a dear friend, and should be a household name with many platinum albums under his belt. Taylor delivers the emotional goods here, and I am always moved when I hear this song. The tempo is a deceptively difficult one, and it's important to lay back and make it feel really relaxed. I'm playing slightly behind the click for most of it and getting to the point where I'm burying the click in the high points to give the feeling of adding energy and urgency (while still nailing the click). As always, I'm looking to build and shape the song, and craft my fills to give them meaning and purpose. Tightening and opening the hats from section to section and oceanic, swiping crashes on the second beats of the choruses are well-calculated and thought out, but add to the overall emotional content. This really is one of my favorite songs.

BRAD:

This pretty ballad has a fairly straight-ahead drum part. One thing I omitted from the transcription of this song is that Todd often drops his stick onto the head after his loud backbeats, lightly buzzing on the snare. I did not notate these because this technique is impossible to notate without it looking as though he is playing an accented buzz or crushed buzz into the head. These buzzes are basically inaudible, so I omitted them.

At bar 16, Todd plays a flam at the beginning of a six-stroke roll, which is a bit unusual for most drummers, though not for Todd. His unaccented snare strokes are very quiet ghost notes and the notated diddles are also very light, providing a touch of extra feel and texture to this laid-back groove.

CENTER OF YOUR HEART

MINUS DRUMS

CONSOLATION PRIZE

TODD:

In "Consolation Prize," we wanted a big scene change between the main riff of the chorus and the verses, and to really use dynamics to give the song a nice shape. For the dreamy verse sections, I go to a second snare drum and a dry flat ride with a rattler on it. I'm thinking about keeping the feel floating and dreamlike. Light comments from crash cymbals are like a splash of cool water against the bone-dry flat ride. The way I'm hitting the second snare is different as well, with many mildly pressed buzzes. The pre-chorus builds tension, and it's back to the regular snare and slightly open hi-hat—and then it's full throttle at the chorus, with an aggressive, washy ride cymbal. The song has a standard form, with some very interesting bass lines in the dreamy sections. It's ultimately a bit of an angry song, so I'm reacting to the ebb and flow of what's happening lyrically as well. Shaping the track with hills and valleys in the dynamics is paramount, while trying to give each section it's own vibe.

BRAD:

Here is another tune by songstress Taylor Mills. Todd uses a second snare drum for the airy verse, and you will notice his signature use of multiple quieter snare notes following an accent, and a lot of snare buzzes under the flat ride. He switches to his main snare and hi-hat at the pre-chorus and chorus, where he really ramps up the energy.

Bars 11 and 12, 33 and 34 (and several other places) reveal a subtle and tasteful musical choice Todd made by omitting the bass drum from the downbeat of alternate measures. I believe he does this to help the groove float more and seem less anchored, which perfectly suits the light, airy verses.

In bars 35 and 44 he plays four very fast thirty-second notes with just his left hand while maintaining the ride pattern. Beginning in bar 61 there is a nice low-key groove that uses a snare buzz over a floor tom note over samba-style bass drum pattern. In this song, it does not sound Latin, but suits the mood of the section and could work in many other songs.

Bars 69 through 72 are just a ripping display of chops that builds into the final chorus perfectly. The inclusion of flams into this fast crescendo pattern is something notable—and ridiculously difficult.

The lick in bar 81 is basically a pattern of quads that Todd fits into the space of a half note. If you want to learn it, ignore the polyrhythmic notation and play eighth note triplet flams between the hands and feet on counts "*3 & ah 4 & ah*," with the hands on "*3 ah &*" and feet playing "*& 4 ah*." Gradually widen the spacing between each note. When everything is perfectly even and "quad-dy", this is the result.

CONSOLATION PRIZE

MINUS DRUMS
Click played as 8s.

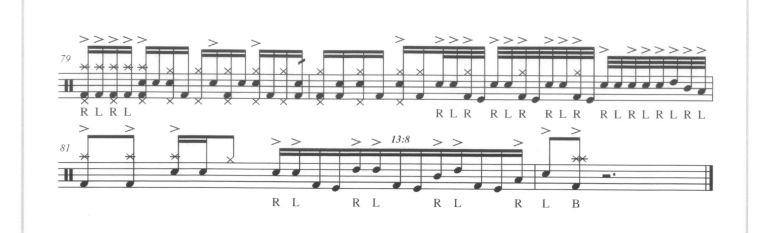

RAVEN

TODD:

"Raven" is a song from a band I was in called The Falling Wallendas in Chicago back in the 1990s. The two records I did with them, *Falling Wallendas* and *Belittle* are two records that I'm fiercely proud of (and you can find them on the internet for pennies). But we thought this track would work for Taylor's record, and we outdid the original. Having Brian Wilson sing in the chorus was pretty sweet too! When originally working up the pattern, I listened to the bass line Scott Bennett was playing, turned off the snares, and started to try to find the right thing. The main form of the song is two bars of 6/8 and one bar of 9/8. This mostly-linear pattern developed with the hi-hat pumping eighth notes, with an alternating open-closed "over ride" that changed the feel every three bars due to the extra beats and the end of the phrases. The open "slosh" on the downbeats become the upbeats 3 bars later, and this continues back and forth though the song. There are a few subtle changes in the feel, with an extra bass drum note in the chorus and an added splash with the backbeat. The outro pattern changes to build with the song as it rides off into the sunset.

BRAD:

Though I was fortunate enough to see the Falling Wallendas perform back in the day, I had never been exactly sure how Todd played this interesting odd-time drum part. In the first two lines of the transcription you can see how the hi-hat splash pattern is displaced for each cycle of the pattern, and this greatly increases the coordination challenges of the piece. The song has several time signature changes occurring throughout that vary from the main form of 6/8, 6/8, and 9/8. Todd drops the snare wires and plays ride bell notes and splash cymbal accents along with his toms, and uses his tom rims for an unusual texture in this very percussive groove.

Hi-Hat Ostinato Resumes

TOGETHER

"Together" is a Styx song from the *Cyclorama* CD that we all wrote in a rehearsal hall one day. I've always liked the summertime feel of this track as well as the conversational phrasing of Tommy Shaw's great lead vocal. The song starts with just guitars and drums, and you'll notice that I'm playing the bell of the hi-hat, and the snare is struck lightly in the center of the drum. For the second part of the first verse (when the bass comes in) there's a light crash, and normal hat and snare activity begin to give it a scene change and help with the build. Part of the bass line is contrapuntal to the bass drum part, which sometimes might not work, but with this track I thought the grounding of the "1" worked nicely with the anticipated bass line. This is a deceptively difficult slow-mid tempo, and it's hard not to push through the bridge, guitar solo, and the ending. It really goes from a whisper to a roar. I'm paying attention to shaping the song, reacting dynamically to the lyrics, utilizing a few motif figures, and really turning this seemingly sleepy song into a party.

BRAD:

Todd begins this one lightly. At bar 14 he switches from hitting the snare head only to playing light rim shots on each backbeat to subtly raise the intensity of the verse. Bar 19 has a useful little fill you might have overlooked. The intensity comes up a bit in bar 22, and then jumps up more after the fill in bar 25. Bar 35 has a nice linear triplet and open hi-hat that he uses to set up the next verse. It is simple but effective. At bar 65 Todd gets a little busier, and the funky groove just percolates with energy. There is a longer pause after the 2/4 measure that is used to make the final chorus' entrance all the more dramatic.

11 TOGETHER

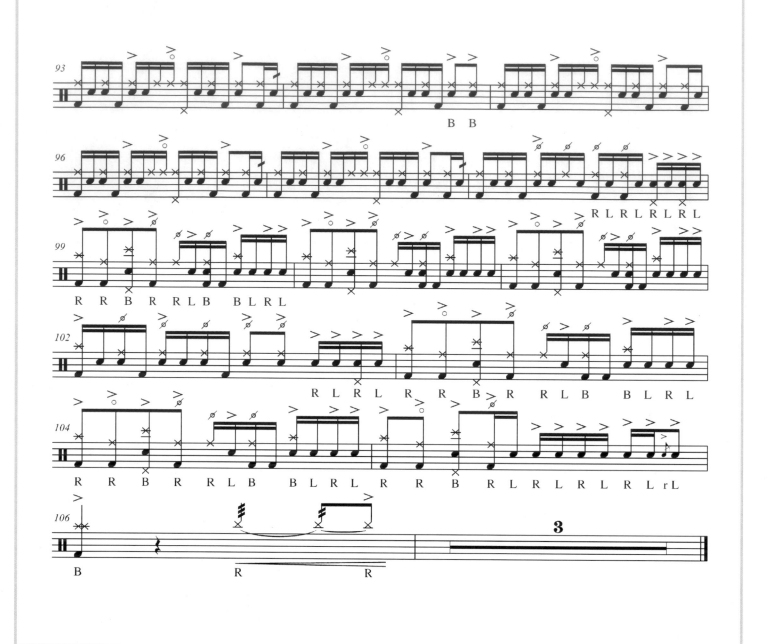

RENEGADE

TODD:

Renegade was originally on Styx's *Pieces of Eight* record from 1978. This has historically been the encore/show closer in the live set, hence the incredibly long fermata at the very end. I've always tried to keep the original flavor of the song intact while adding lots of drum activity that does not distract or get in the way of the essence of the piece. Lots of ghost notes appear throughout, and it's important to keep the energy driving with a sense of urgency and purpose.

BRAD:

The intro of this one has a four-on-the-floor bass drum pattern and a funky, swung hand pattern on top. Todd breaks out of the quarter-note bass drum feel in a few places, and each time he does the groove gets even funkier: check out bars 18 and 21-24. When he moves to the ride, he emphasizes the "*&'s*" and the "*& ah*" of beat 3 on the bell, which again adds a bit more funk to the steady quarter-note bass drum pattern.

At bar 47 Todd gets busier on the ride, playing a fast shuffle pattern (remember these are swung 16ths). However, at bar 54 he plays a 16th-note snare fill that is not swung—but the beat after it is. At bar 63 the feel straightens out again for the dramatic breakdown section. In this section it almost sounds as if there is a snare echo. Todd slams a loud snare hit on the backbeats and bounces a lighter note immediately after causing this effect. Bar 66 has powerful paradiddle-diddle into a bass drum and gong-bass triplet embellishment.

The time signature switches to cut time in bar 79 resulting in a double-time feel. Todd uses a back-and-forth Ringo-esque hand motion for the beginning part of this. He adds some double-bass triplets, and now the eighth notes become swung. He continues to embellish the groove with more and more triplets and double bass, increasing the excitement of the section. At bar 135 he launches into a double bass shuffle with his left foot playing the downbeats and his right foot playing the "*ah's*," as many drummers raised on jazz will do. The rubato double-bass fermata begins at bar 150 and is long enough that it could almost be considered another drum solo. Interesting drum flurries abound, so if you are a double bass player looking for new licks, this is a treasure trove.

RENEGADE

Swing 1/16th Notes

SOLO TRANSCRIPTIONS

SOLOING ON A MOTIF

TODD:

I originally stumbled on this motif when recording a drum loop CD in LA back in 2000 called *More Than Styx*. I remembered the basic riff even though the feel did not make it onto the CD. It was an interesting landscape to explore, to see how the motif could develop and evolve with the different snare sounds. On the downbeat of the main motif (7-note figure) section, it's important to nail the snare with the left hand along with the hi-hat on the right, and double that left hand quickly to smear it into a smooth-sounding roll.

BRAD:

This solo uses three different snare drums. The two auxiliary snares located to the left of Todd's hi-hat are notated with black and white triangular note heads and the snares are turned off. The main figure is a septuplet with seven notes played in the space of the first beat. This is played as an accented "tap roll" (RLLRRLL). This figure is embellished with a variety of fills until the first section change that occurs in bar 33.

Todd transitions into this section with a clever triplet hi-hat lick that uses a hi-hat closure to maintain the continuous flow of notes. He uses a couple of variations on this technique in bars 40 and 49. He returns to the original motif again, but this time he plays it off his auxiliary hi-hat and starts embellishing it with faster five stroke rolls. He throws an extended fill in at bar 85 that consists of a quick quintuplet pattern that sounds a bit like a repeated triplet. The note after the auxiliary hi-hat note is softer, because it is the last note of a fast left-handed triple-stroke.

The next scene change occurs at bar 105, where Todd plays a tom groove that could be useful in many situations. He returns to another half-time groove (with the snare accent on 3) briefly before throwing in some very challenging polyrhythmic patterns beginning in bar 119. While maintaining a steady eighth-note pulse on his hi-hat, Todd's bass drum and snare play a triplet rhythm against it, creating a 2-over-3 feel. Crazier still, a few bars later he plays a quintuplet against the hi-hat pulse, resulting in a 4-over-5 pattern. In bar 127 there is another version of a quintuplet that's played twice as fast that is actually is a tad easier than the previous one, though the term "easy" is relative in this case.

At bar 145 Todd shifts gears using a metric modulation based on accented half-note triplets. A metric modulation sounds like a tempo change, but it actually uses a different note value to achieve its effect. The way Todd does this is to base his implied tempo on a triplet, shifting his snare and bass patterns accordingly and making the music feel like it has slowed down. His accents suggest half-note triplets because he is emphasizing every fourth note of the triplet, resulting in a 4-over-3 effect. Had Todd emphasized every other note of the triplet (which again would be easier since 3-over-2 is easier than 4-over-3), the groove would have felt as though it sped up.

The next section is based on the baião, which is a style of Brazilian music. When adapted to the drum set, baião usually has the foot pattern Todd is playing, with the bass drum landing on counts "*1 ah (2) & 3 ah (4) &*" and the hi-hat playing all the "*&'s.*" Todd solos on top of this, bending the note values but leaving the feet locked in place. By bending the time over the steady foot pattern, he gives the impression of two or more drummers playing together, much like a timbalero soloing over his fellow percussionists, alternately pushing and pulling the feel. This is very difficult to learn and takes years to master.

At bar 277 Todd shifts to a funk groove section with lots of nice things worth adopting. For some of this he uses a constant 16th-note hand motion and moves his hands between the snare and hi-hat, embellishing with rolls, drags, and accents. Bars 290 and 298 shift gears to include a couple of amazing triplet fills. For the outro he repeats the main motif, putting musical bookends on this incredible piece.

13 SOLOING ON A MOTIF

Snares Off Auxiliary Snare Drums

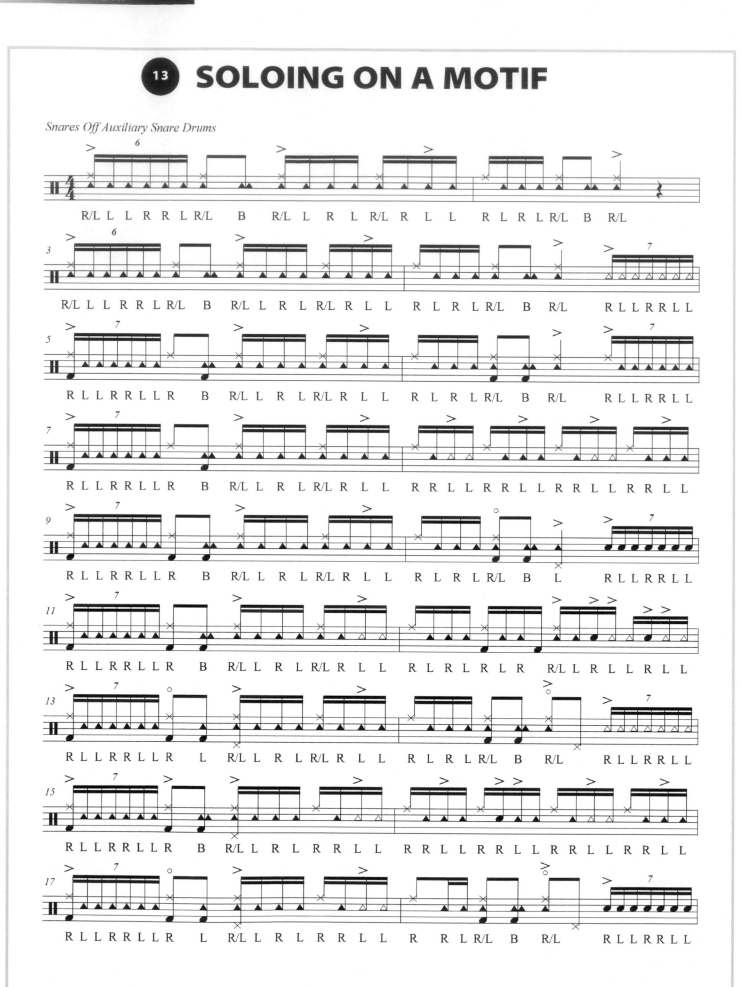

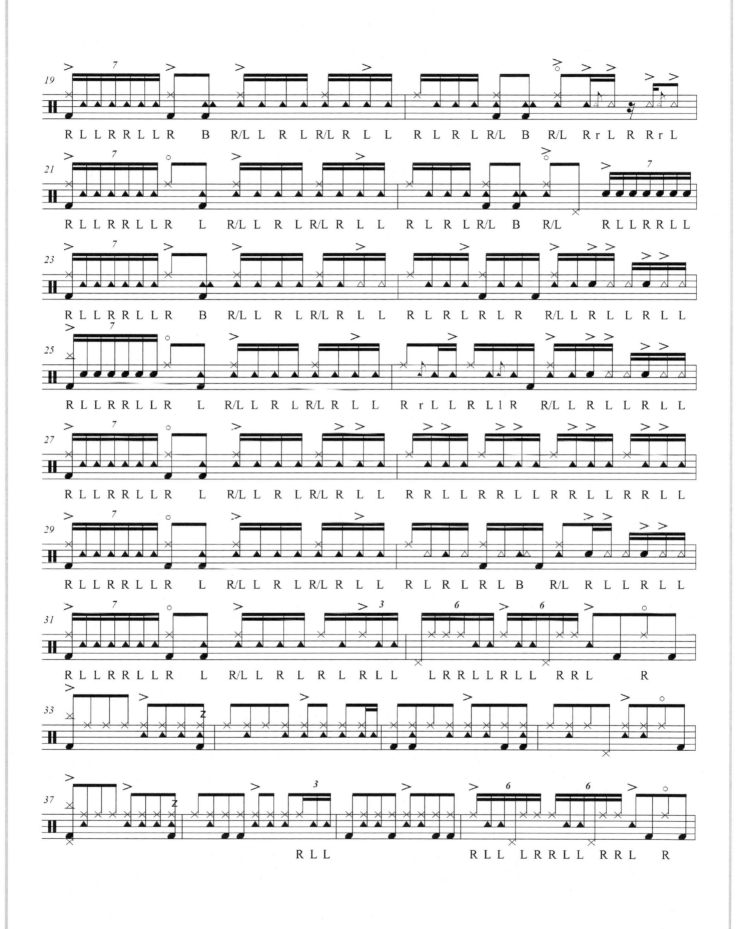

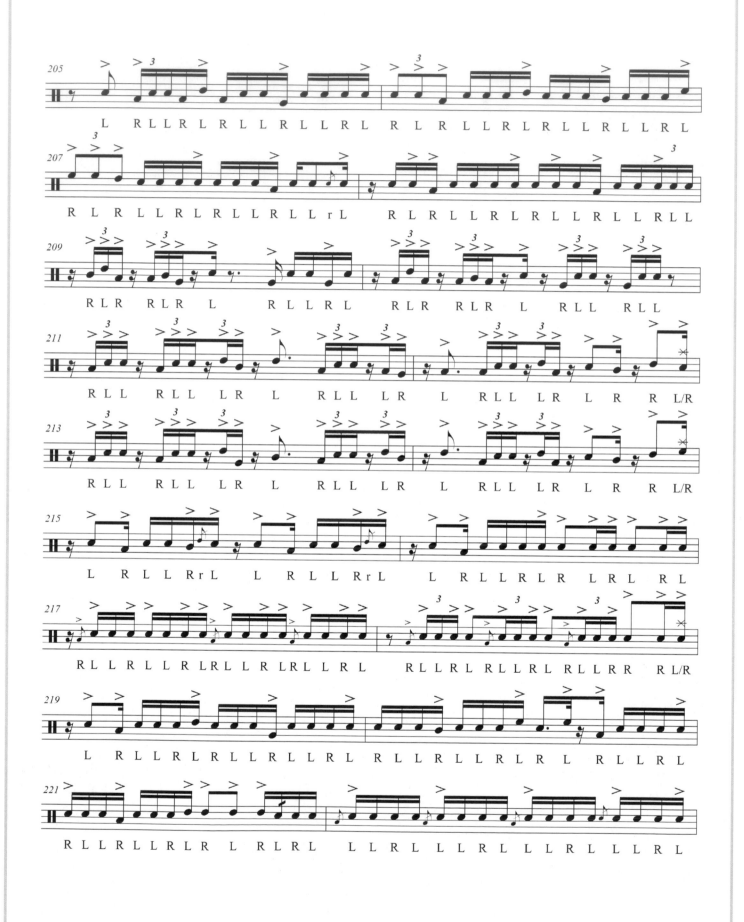

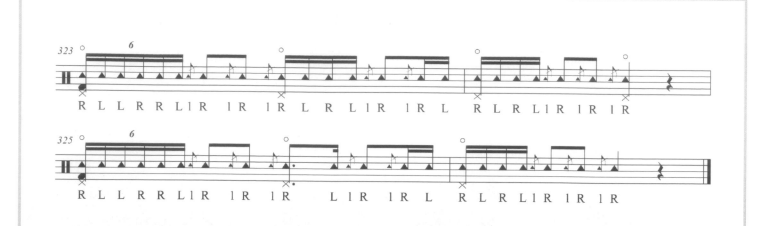

CLIFF SHOT SOLO

TODD:

We set up for the outside sunrise shots after sleeping only an hour. It was around 5:30am, and this was after four days of continuous filming. We knew we wanted to capture the scenery but I hadn't thought for a moment of what I was going to play. My partner in the DVD project, Eric Dorris, told me to "just play." So everything that was filmed here was a total musical stream-of-consciousness fueled by the delirium of little to no sleep. I played for about 40 minutes straight without stopping on that cold December day. Sometimes going out on a limb and being a bit delirious can yield interesting results.

BRAD:

This solo uses a few variations of a funky Latin baião groove that begins with the bass drum on "*1 & ah*," and the snare plays the "*&*" of 2 for a tumbao-like pattern. Bars 17 and 18 have a very nice triplet embellishment that is made more challenging because Todd voices it between his snare and kick, and then plays it over his hi-hat creating a brief 3-over-2 polyrhythm.

A couple of bars later Todd plays a fast sextuplet between his bass drum and high tom that is fast enough to sound like a roll. He accents his right hand on the bell of his middle ride cymbal, which would be an especially good idea were he playing this with other musicians, as if to say, "Here's the quarter note!"

Bars 22 and 23 have a great Latin funk groove which is worth learning because it could work in lots of other tunes. Bars 24 and 32 have one of my favorite fills in this solo. Todd plays a flam pattern between his ride, high tom and snare that echoes the baião bass drum pattern. Bar 28 has another one of those sextuplet roll licks, but this time his left hand moves around the kit. There is another fast sextuplet pattern starting in bar 40, which is based around a linear triplet.

Bars 43 through 45 feel like Todd changes to triplets, although actually he performs a brief metric modulation here. By playing a shuffle pattern with the bass drum, snare, and ride over the eighth-note hi-hat pattern he creates a 3-over-2 polyrhythm. However, this shuffle is not played in triplets; he continues playing 16th notes, cleverly shifting the perception of time before returning to the original time feel.

The very last bar of the solo has a triplet flam fill that would work well in many other spots.

14 CLIFF SHOT SOLO

4am FREE FORM JAZZ SOLO

TODD:

This solo was actually played at 4 am. We filmed a few of the small kit segments in those late hours, had a brief nap, and then set up for the outdoor sunrise shots. I don't remember much from this period of filming; it was all stream-of-consciousness playing. It's incredible to me that our illustrious transcriber, Brad Schlueter, could actually make sense of this, since the time was completely free.

BRAD:

This solo is played *rubato*, meaning freely and at the whim of the performer, or simply without a consistent tempo. If anyone ever accuses you of rushing or dragging, just say you were playing *rubato*. They will still think your meter needs work, but at least they will know you are educated.

Seriously though, this type of stream-of-consciousness soloing can often spark creative ideas that you would not discover otherwise. Often we have unconscious rules that govern our playing and practicing. Turning that internal censor off can help you become truly improvisational and open your mind to fresh possibilities.

Since Todd's speeds shift up and down, I tried to approximate the note values as best I could. Since the whole thing ebbs and flows, a notated 16th note at the beginning of the solo might not be exactly the same speed as one near the end. Todd's transitions from one note value to another are often incremental hurrying and dragging as opposed to abruptly changing from one speed to another.

There are a lot of paradiddle-diddles, paradiddles and other rudimental stickings used in the solo. Linear triplets voiced off the ride cymbal make their first appearance at the beginning of bar 3. Todd plays some jarring flams broken between his ride, bass drum, and snare in bars 7, 13, and elsewhere. There are some 32nd-note ruffs played off his bass drum, tom, and snare first seen in bar 11. One of the things he does throughout this solo is break double strokes across two instruments such as ride and low tom (seen in bar 37). Of course, all of these techniques can be used in meter to spice up your jazz solos too.

15 4am FREE FORM JAZZ SOLO

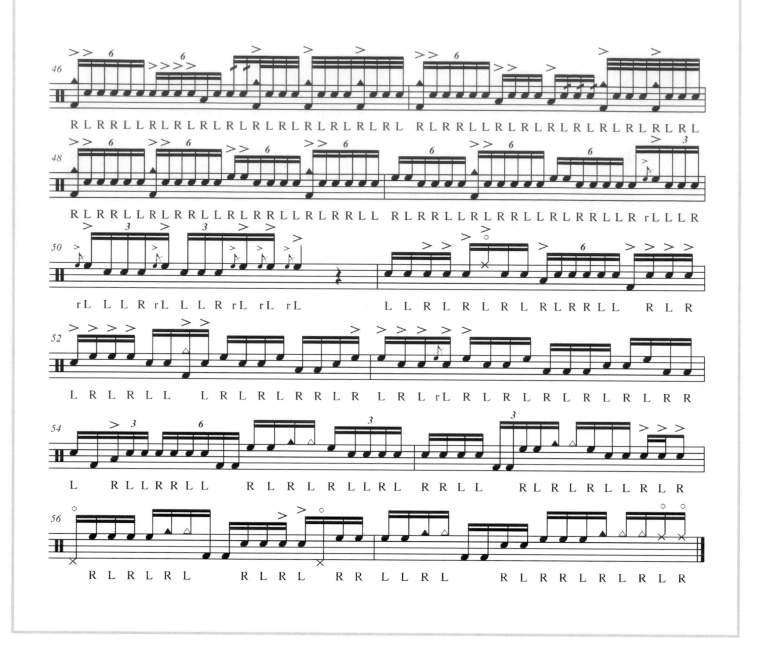

CARNIVAL SAMBA SOLO

TODD:

This is my take on what a street carnival sounds like. I certainly can't say it's authentic, but I did not grow up with this idiosyncratic music as my cultural experience. There's more than one way to skin a cat, and more than one way to play a samba. A lot of rhythmic bending is taking place—blurring the line between straight and swung notes. I'm also thinking about the unique "lope" that a samba feel has, and I'm trying to replicate that throughout.

BRAD:

Todd begins this one with a series of syncopated fills on his snares played with the wires off. He emphasizes a lot of the "e's" and "ah's," bending the rhythms to create a killer opening for this solo. He plays his tom rim, getting a sound reminiscent of the shell of a timbale for the opening groove, and uses buzzes and double strokes for added textures. Todd's bass drum pattern is unique and reminds me of a cross between a samba and a surdo pattern landing on "ah 2" and "ah 4." At bar 13, he switches his foot ostinato to a standard samba groove, but uses his floor tom to suggest the surdo part on beats 2 and 4. The main hi-hat and auxiliary hi-hat are gradually introduced, along with drags and flams, which requires some impressive coordination and chops. Bar 24 has a brief but killer snare fill. At bar 50, Todd begins playing some really quick and interesting hand patterns using triplets and bursts of singles. Then, at bar 65, he plays eighth-note quintuplets over the samba, and by bar 73 begins pushing and pulling the rhythms, which sounds incredible (but results in some crazy-looking notation). Bar 88 is reminiscent of the syncopated fills he opened this solo with. In bar 125, he returns to the opening groove, and throws a nice sextuplet fill into the groove at bar 131. Todd gradually gets softer and moves both hands over to the hi-hat to finish this piece.

16 CARNIVAL SAMBA SOLO

25
B r L L R L R B R L R L R L R B B r L L R L R B R L R r L R L R B B r L L R L R B R L R r L R L R B
28
l Rr L L R L R B R L Rr L R L R B R L Rr L R L R B R L Rr L R L R B R L Rr L R L R B Rr Lr L R L R B
31
R L Rr L R L R B R L Rr L R L R B R L Rr L R L R B Rr Lr L R L R R B B R L R B B B B R L R B
34
B B R L R B B B B R L R B B B R L R B B B B R L R B R L B R L R B R L B R L R B
37
B B R L R B B B B R L R B B B R L R B B B B B R L R B B B R L R B B B B R L R B
40
R L B R L R B R L B R L R B R L R B R L R B R L Rr L R L R B R L R B R L Rr L R L R B R L R B
43
B r L L R L R B R L R B R L R L R B B L R B B L R B B L R B R L B L R L R B R L R B R L R B
46
R rL R L R B R L R B R L Rr L R L R B R L R B R L Rr L R L R B
48
R L L R L R L L R L R L L R L R L L R L R L L R L R L L R L R L L R L R L L R L

THANKS, MR. SMITH

TODD:

Steve Smith's drum solo from the live Journey album *Captured* is one of the all-time classic rock drum solos. I was lucky to have taped another show from that 1980 tour off the radio, so I had a whole different version to listen to while I was growing up. This solo piece is loosely based around the double bass shuffle of this famous solo. We all have "big bang" moments that inspire us as drummers— whether you saw Ringo on the Ed Sullivan Show, or remember the first time you saw a drumset up close—and one of my biggest moments was seeing Steve play on that 1980 tour. This solo is my humble attempt at honoring someone whose playing meant so much to me. On his *Drumset Technique/History of the US Beat* DVD, Steve dedicated a solo to the great Tony Williams, and called it "Thanks, Mr. Williams." So this is called "Thanks, Mr. Smith."

BRAD:

I wrote most of this solo in 12/8 since it has a predominately compound (triplet) feel, but wrote other sections of it in 4/4, when the feel shifts to a simple (duple) feel. Todd begins with a shuffle based on a Swiss army triplet—though with the flams played flat (both hands in unison). He adds the bass drum and then starts embellishing this groove with flams and drags. Bars 8, 12, and 16 show how good Todd's hands are. In these bars he plays accented triplet fills with only his left hand, while maintaining the right-handed shuffle—just like Steve Smith does today in his solos. The hi-hat usually outlines the triplet feel, but Todd varies the bass drum pattern from the main feel playing 3-against-2 in bar 20 and an Afro-Cuban bembe in bar 27. Bar 24 has a ripping fill that (fortunately for the rest of us) will sound great even when played slower.

In bar 31, Todd plays a linear pattern between his right foot and hands that fits four notes into the space of three eighth notes (and in 12/8 time). This artificial division is called a quadruplet (much like a triplet is an artificial division in 4/4 time). I used the 4:3 ratio above these to keep things clear for those less familiar with reading 12/8 time. These patterns sound really incredible interspersed among the triplet patterns.

At bar 55, Todd accents every fourth note on his auxiliary hi-hat creating an ear-grabbing 4-over-3 effect.

Bar 70 has another interesting variation on the fill from bar 24; this time Todd extends it by playing quads, resulting in a 4-over-6 feel. Several more variations of this idea occur in bars 76, 120, and 127. At bar 81 we see him play a very cool shuffle pattern with a triple-stroked backbeat. There's another ripping pattern in bar 111. This one comes across as a 9-over-2 feel but he plays the bass drums more as written than wider and slurred.

Bar 165 sees the time signature switch to 4/4, and this certainly makes more sense with the jazz-fusion baião pattern that Todd plays here. (Reading that in 12/8 would be a nightmare.) There are some pretty insane quad-type double bass fills leading into the feel change at bar 238. Todd swings the 16th notes on these funky grooves and briefly brings the volume down with a rim-click beat before tearing into another double bass triplet groove. At bar 274 he plays a very visual triplet pattern that is basically the flam accent rudiment played between the snare and crash cymbal. He ends this amazing solo with a quick flurry of double bass and crash cymbals.

17 THANKS, MR. SMITH

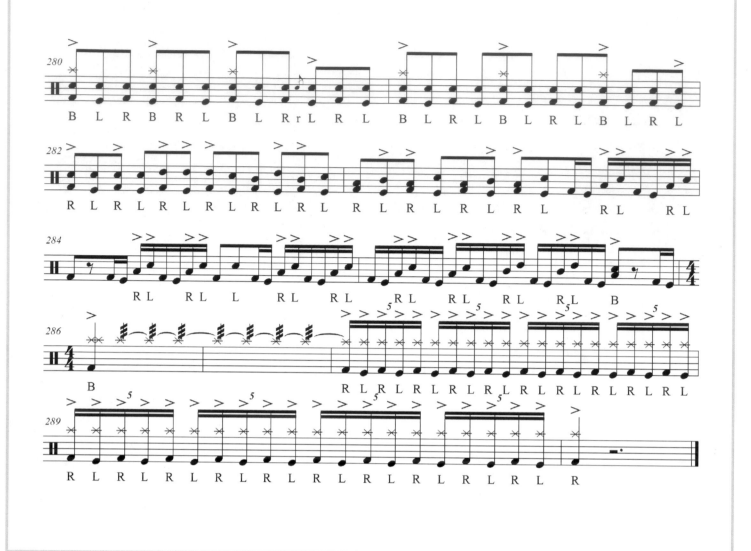

LESSONS - DOUBLE BASS DRUMS

I get asked about the double bass drums a lot, but really in recent years I haven't really paid much attention to them, or really worked on them. When I was 12 or 13 years old, I was really listening to a lot of Steve Smith, Terry Bozzio, and Simon Phillips, and those guys were kind of my templates for double bass. I never really got into anything fancy other than R-L-R-L stuff. I play mostly heel-up and kind of slide up the pedal.

1.

I'm just muscling that out, there's really nothing fancy going on downstairs like multi-strokes (double stroke rolls, heel-toe technique). Double bass is something I've maintained and that works well in the context of arena rock (like playing with Styx), especially for ending the songs.

I always had this little system that was just however many notes on top with the hands over however many notes with the feet.

So two-and-two on one bass drum is:

2.

Two-and-two with two bass drums is:

3.

What I'm trying do there when I'm playing them fast is really muscle them out and get a nice level between the top and the bottom. I've seen people play them like their arms are noodles. If you're going to pull out that lick, you need to muscle it out. It's not just playing loudly, you need to articulate the notes and work at getting a nice balance between the top and the bottom.

It's just my opinion, but it always drove me crazy if I saw a drummer end a 2-and-2 fill ("quads") with a snare and a crash. As a kid I thought, "Why not add three bass drum notes at the end and come out with a bass drum and a crash?"

4.

Let's change the numbers and go 3 on the top and 2 on the bottom.

5.

Being that it's five notes it can work as a sort of 4-over-3 in a groove.

6.

Exercise

Brad: Todd's feet play on approximately every other eighth note of an eighth-note triplet, creating a polyrhythmic feel. He plays these figures very evenly so it's actually a bit closer to septuplets; hence the notation. The third line shows Todd playing a longer fill that has 27 notes spaced over four beats, ending on beat 3. There are other ways I could have written it, but this conveys how Todd phrases it, and somehow the notes manage to fit into the space.

Here's a challenging exercise that can help you learn to play this lick. Start with this sextuplet pattern and then squeeze an extra note into it, creating septuplets, while striving to play all the notes with completely even spacing.

Todd Tip: Always be aware of where your rhythmic resolution point is. Once you start a lick, you have to be able to get out of it.

Now, let's take four notes on the top with the hands and two on the bottom, creating a six-note figure.

7.

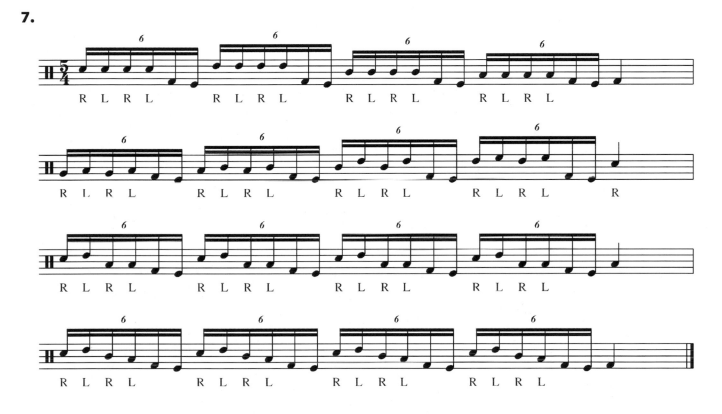

We could add a three-note conjunction:

8. Three-note conjunction

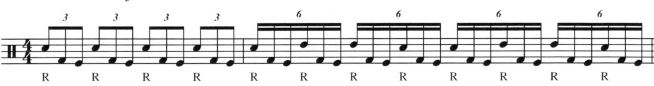

Now we have a nine-note combination.

9.   Nine Note Conjunction

That leaves the other arm free where you could actually play a cymbal.

10.

You could also start the four (on the top) on an "&":

11.

You can combine a four-and-two with a two-and-two.

12.

R L   R L   R L   R L R L   R L R L   R L   R L

R L R L   R L   R L   R L R L   R L   R

And so on, and so on, ad nauseum.

Todd Sucherman Hybrid Rudiments

I'd like to spend a little bit of time showing you how I apply some of the rudiments to the drumset.

HALF-PARADIDDLE

Paradiddles and inverted paradiddles can be used by themselves, as conjunctions in longer passages, or you can use just half of a paradiddle. The half-paraddidle can also be phrased as 4-over-3.

1. Half-Paradiddle   Half-Paradiddle in a 4:3 Rhythm

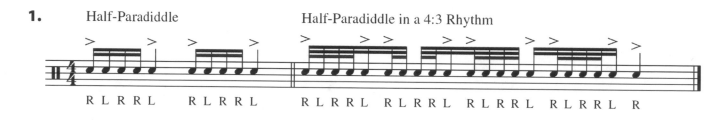

R L R R L   R L R R L   R L R R L   R L R R L   R L R R L   R L R R L   R

And that was just a couple of orchestrations. You can go nuts expounding upon that idea.

2. Half Paradiddle used in 4-over-3 rhythm

R L R R L R L R R L R L R R L R L R R L R L R L   R L R R L R L L R L R R L R L L R L R R L R

L L R L R R L R L L R L R R L R L R R L R L R R   L R L R R L R L R R L R L R R L R L R R L

You could do it with an inverted half-paradiddle (with the diddle in the middle).

3. Inverted Half-Paradiddle   Inverted Half-Paradiddle in a 4:3 Rhythm

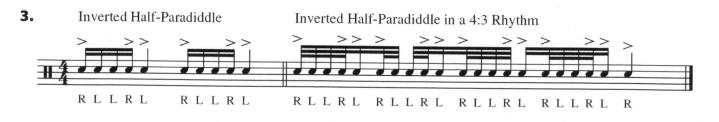

R L L R L   R L L R L   R L L R L   R L L R L   R L L R L   R L L R L   R

The rhythm would be the same, but if you kept your right hand on the toms, that same 4:3 idea at the same rate would sound like this:

4.

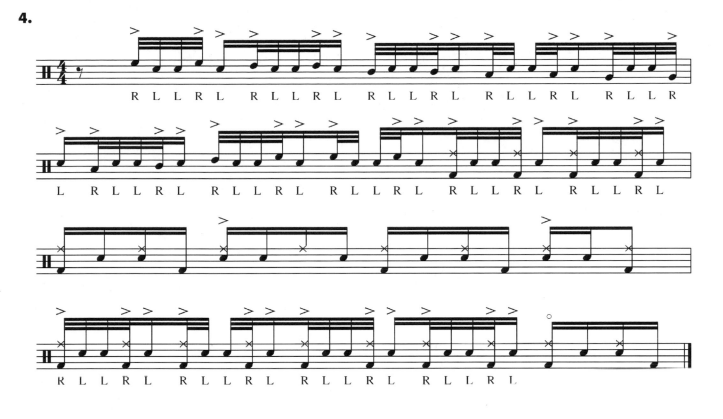

INVERTED PARADIDDLES

There's a lot you can do with inverted paradiddles. The sticking is:

5.   Inverted Paradiddles

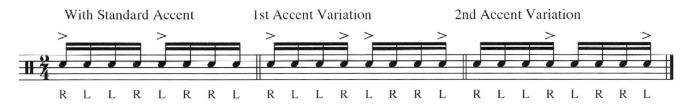

If I put my right hand on the hi-hat and left hand on the snare, it sounds like a hipper groove than the regular paradiddle. I'll be changing the accents and the hills and valleys to give things a different shape, so it's not just a machine gun sound.

6.

Now I could also use that as a groove, putting the right hand on the ride cymbal and left hand on the hi-hat.

7.

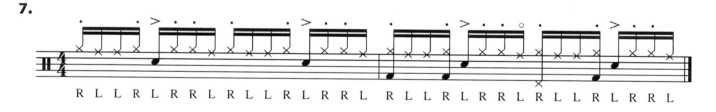

Here's a short solo using this concept.

8.

So really, I like to take one idea and try and see how many different things I can come up with on the drumset. That only adds to the vocabulary that you can call upon. If you can take one idea and come up with ten variations on it, and do that for every idea you have, then your toolbox will grow very quickly.

SIX STROKE ROLLS

Let's take a moment to look at six-stroke rolls. These can be played at a sextuplet rate or a bit more militaristic and stiff.

9. Six-stroke roll sextuplet version   Marching Version

This rudiment is used for classic Motown intros like "Ain't Too Proud To Beg" by the Temptations.

10.

You can take the accents and orchestrate them on the toms beginning with the right or left hand. You can also start with the left hand and bring in the cymbals and add bass drums on the main accents, as well doing the same basic thing but starting with the right hand.

11.

Right-hand lead

Left-hand lead

Left-hand lead with cymbals and bass drum

Right-hand lead with hi-hat, toms and bass drum

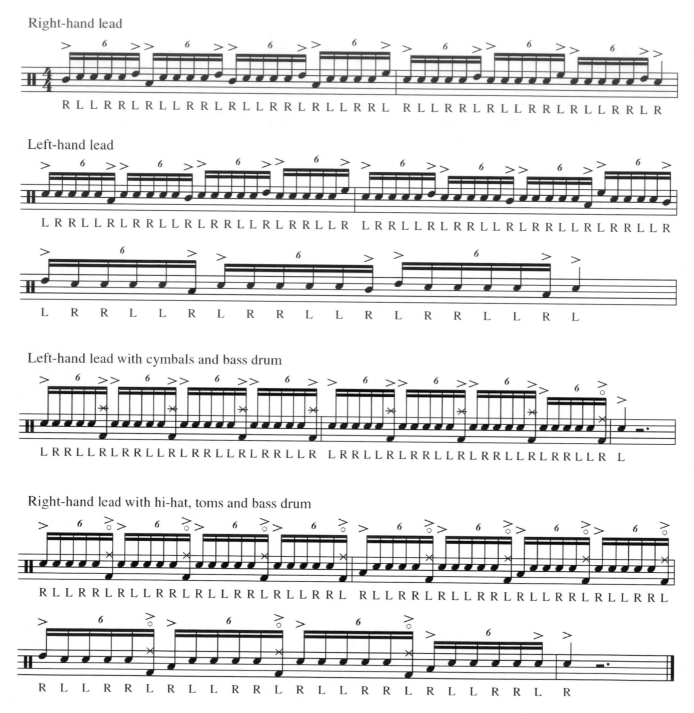

PARADIDDLE-DIDDLES

Another six-note figure is the paradiddle-diddle. This could played either at the sextuplet rate or the 4-over-3 rate.

12.

Paradiddle-diddles in sextuplets   Paradiddle-diddles at the 4-over-3 rate

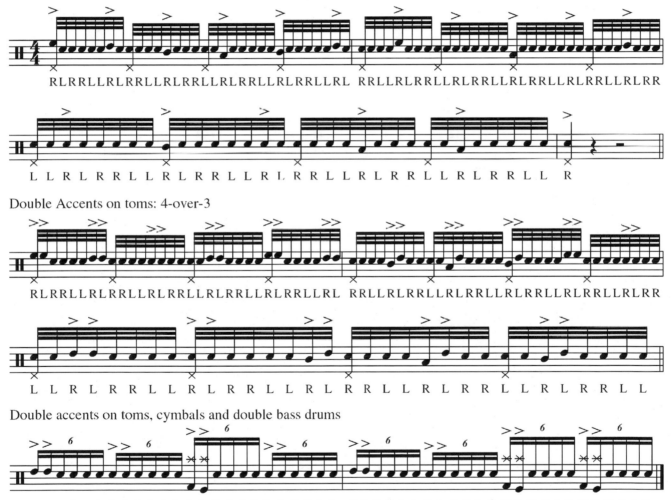

RLRRLLRLRRLLRLRRLLRLRRLL   RLRRLLRLRRLLRLRRLLRLRRLLR

We can move it around the kit with the first note on the toms (or the first two notes on the toms). We can also get the bass drum and cymbals involved.

13.

Accents on toms: 4-over-3

RLRRLLRLRRLLRLRRLLRLRRLLRL RRLLRLRRLLRLRRLLRLRRLLRLRRLLRLRR

LLRLRRLLRLRRLLRLRRLLRLRRLLRLRRLL R

Double Accents on toms: 4-over-3

RLRRLLRLRRLLRLRRLLRLRRLLRL RRLLRLRRLLRLRRLLRLRRLLRLRRLLRLRR

LLRLRRLLRLRRLLRLRRLLRLRRLLRLRRLL

Double accents on toms, cymbals and double bass drums

RLRRLLRLRRLLRLRRLLRLRRLL RLRRLLRLRRLLRLRRLLRLRRLL

They can be made into their own groove.

14.

You could take that sticking and orchestrate in a slower groove.

15.

What would happen if we were to add a bass drum note and make it a seven-note grouping? This has been a very popular fusion fill for a long time. You could have the bass drum be the pick-up note or place it on the downbeat. You can add conjunctions to it as well, to lengthen the grouping.

16.

Bass drum as pick-up note

Bass drum as downbeat

Adding conjunctions

Now let's add two bass drum notes and make it an eight-note grouping.

17.

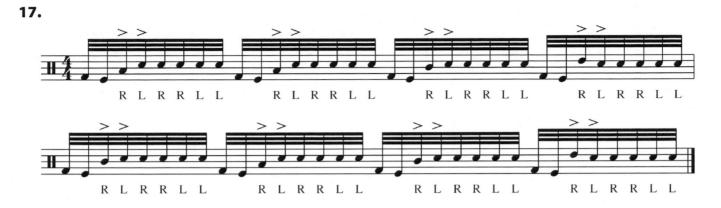

Let's look at flam accents and pataflaflas on the kit. I'm going to flatten them out (play flams as unisons).

18.

Flat Pataflafla   Flat Flam Accent

Now I'll try and think of little tom tom melodies while phrasing the flam accents in groups of five, seven, and nine.

19.

Here are two variations on Swiss army triplets. These use alternating stickings.

20.

If you put the flam on the last triplet, you get that Tony Williams thing.

21.

R L r L R L r L R L r L R L r L R L r L R L r L R L r L R L r L

R L r L R L r L R L r L r L r L R L r L R L r L R L r L r L r L r L

This is one of my favorite licks of all time. Some people call it the "Tony Williams lick," and some people call it the "blushda." I always called it the "ga-blush" because that's what it sounds like to me. The secret's been out on this lick for many years now. I first stumbled across this lick around 1982 after hearing it on a Vital Information record. As soon as I figured it out, I was so thrilled because I had been mystified by it. Back then there were only a handful of guys I heard play it: Vinnie Colaiuta, Tony Williams, and Steve Smith. But today, many drummers use it in a one-dimensional way.

Here's the basic blushda. One interesting variation is to leave the right hand on the tom. It's often played as 4-over-3; here's that phrasing with a groove. Also, if you do it with a right flam, it leaves your right hand open to play some other things. Whichever way you do it, by adding in a couple comments from the left hand you can change the shape of it.

22.

What if we kept the right hand on the hi-hat? We could add a bass drum to get a nice flam between it and the snare drum. We could use that in a groove. You could phrase a blushda in five. You could even play it with your feet on double bass.

23.

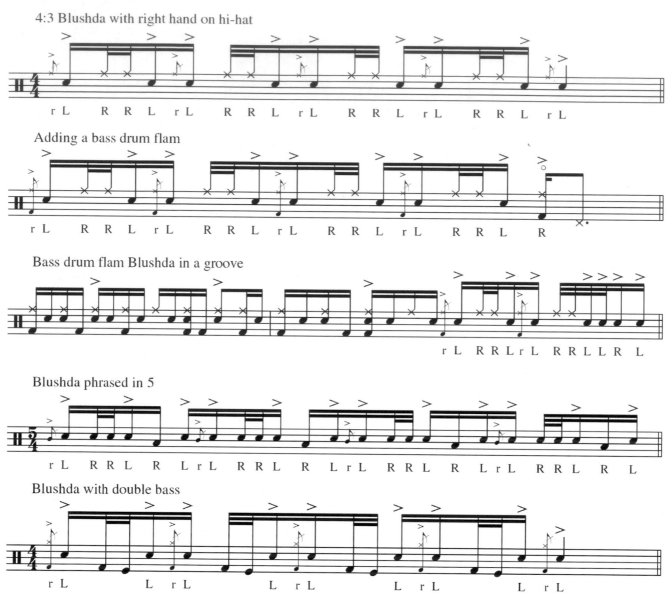

4:3 Blushda with right hand on hi-hat

Adding a bass drum flam

Bass drum flam Blushda in a groove

Blushda phrased in 5

Blushda with double bass

FLAM ROLLS

Here's a little bit on flam rolls. They're good at filling out a beat. It just adds a little more density, something different than using the six-stroke roll in a Motown context, for instance. Little things like this can fill out a beat and make it feel fat and wide. This leads me into what I call the straight ga-blush, which is the Tony Williams lick to me, but played in four. If you open it up and stretch it a little bit you get sextuplets. Again, this is a really aggressive lick. What happens if you orchestrate it in different ways? What if you were to leave your right hand on a tom?

24.

You get the point. The main message is to take these rudiments that you've worked out on a pad, put them on the drumset, and try to orchestrate them in different ways. Use your imagination and creativity and just let it run wild, and have fun exploring what you can come up with. These ideas are just things that I came up with, or learned from other people. If you play it the way you play, it becomes yours. These are just templates for you to take and come up with your own ideas and phrases.

CONCLUSION

I'd like to thank you for buying this book. It has been a pleasure and a privilege to provide some ideas and guidance to help you on your journey. It's important to always remember to have fun. Music is not a contest or a sport; music is art. You have to forge ahead with all your being if you want to do this for a living. But if you don't end up doing this for a living, be involved with drumming. Be involved with music. Be involved with art. Create! It's one of life's greatest joys and rewards. Find your thing, whether it's drums, guitar, painting, sculpting, knitting, or whatever. And as a dear friend of mine once said, "Stay up late for your thing." Be a patron of the arts. Pull yourself away from the TV screen or computer screen and go out and experience live music. Support live music. The arts are in danger in so many school systems, it's downright terrifying. Expose young kids to music and the arts early and often. Well, you've made it this far into the book, so that tells me that you're obviously committed to drumming, so you know how cathartic and therapeutic it is. I know for me, I can go into my drum room at 3 o'clock and begin to play, and seemingly 20 minutes later it's 6 o'clock. What an amazing out-of-body experience it is. What a beautiful thing! If everybody in the world had *something like that* in their lives, man, what a different and better world it would be.

Todd Sucherman thanks:

ACKNOWLEDGMENTS:

Todd would like to thank:

Victor Salazar for introducing me to Eric Dorris.

Eric Dorris for his painstaking and groundbreaking work making *Methods and Mechanics.*

Scott Cavendar, Nathan Batiste, and JR Taylor for their work on the DVD.

STYX band, crew, and management for everything.

Jerry Goodman for his genius.

Scott Bennett for his amazing songs and musicianship.

Allen Keller for "Raven."

All my friends at Pearl Drums, Sabian Cymbals, Pro Mark Drumsticks, Remo Drumheads, Toca Percussion, and Audix Microphones.

Rob Wallis, Paul Siegel, Joe Bergamini and everyone at Hudson Music.

And to Brad Schlueter for your dedication to this project. Thanks for your astounding work and for your friendship.

DEDICATED TO:

My father who taught me to play.

My mother who let me play.

My brothers, who were incredible and joyous to play with.

My wife, Taylor, who is everything to me.

Brad Schlueter thanks:

Todd Sucherman for his friendship, inspirational playing, and this rewarding opportunity.

Jim Streich for his friendship and for making the Drum Pad such a great place to teach. Victor Salazar, Ben Hornor, Tommy Levandoski, John Maloney, Greg Rapp, Chris Cash, Tammy Peden, and everyone else at the Drum Pad for making it an interesting and fun place while graciously enduring my incessant practicing through student absences.

Andy Doerschuk, Dave Constantin, Phil and Connie Hood at Drum! Magazine for giving me the opportunity to continue to develop my transcribing and writing skills every month for the past decade.

Scot Ashley, Doug Ackman, Chris Block, Dean Radzik, John Periaswamy, and Jeff Decker for their friendship and humor.

Joe Bergamini, Rick Gratton, Rob Wallis, Paul Siegel, Mike Hoff, and everyone at Hudson Music for taking the chance.

My friends at *Modern Drummer, Electronic Musician, Gearwire, Thomann Websites,* and *JazzTimes* for employing me as a writer or transcriber at various times.

I especially thank my wonderful Aimee, who has made her own share of sacrifices while I was consumed with this project.

DEDICATED TO:

My mother and father who always loved and inspired me.

For more information check out:
www.ToddSucherman.com
www.BradSchlueter.com

MUSIC CREDITS

"TEARS OF JOY"
Written by Jerry Goodman
Amory Music/Listening Room Music (ASCAP)
Admin. Sony ATV Music Publishing

"ONE WITH EVERYTHING"
Written by Tommy Shaw, James Young, Todd Sucherman, Lawrence Gowan, Glen Burtnik

Tranquility Base Songs (ASCAP), Canis Indomitus Music (ASCAP), Bubinga Freak Music (ASCAP), Gowan Publishing (SOCAN)

"TOGETHER"
Written by Tommy Shaw, James Young, Todd Sucherman, Lawrence Gowan, Glen Burtnik

Tranquility Base Songs (ASCAP), Canis Indomitus Music (ASCAP), Bubinga Freak Music (ASCAP), Gowan Publishing (SOCAN)

"ANYTHING"
Written by Scott Bennett
Fur Vest Music (BMI), Ted and Moose Music (BMI)

"CENTER OF YOUR HEART"
Written by Scott Bennett
Fur Vest Music (BMI), Ted and Mose Music (BMI)

"CONSOLATION PRIZE"
Written by Scott Bennett
Fur Vest Music (BMI), Ted and Moose Music (BMI)

"RAVEN"
Written by Scott Bennett, Allen Keller
Fur Vest Music (BMI), Chang & Eng Music (ASCAP),
Ted and Moose Music (BMI), Bubinga Freak Music (ASCAP)

"RENEGADE"
Written by Tommy Shaw
Almo Music/Stygian Songs (ASCAP)